GREAT ILLUSTRATED CLASSICS

LITTLE WOMEN

Louisa May Alcott

adapted by
Lucia Monfried

Illustrations by
Pablo Marcos Studio

BARONET BOOKS

BARONET BOOKS, New York, New York

GREAT ILLUSTRATED CLASSICS

**edited by
Malvina G. Vogel**

CONTENTS

About the Author

Louisa May Alcott was born in 1832, the second daughter of four. Her father, A. Bronson Alcott, was an idealistic educator and philosopher. She spent most of her life in Boston and nearby Concord, Massachusetts.

Seeing how hard her mother had to work, Louisa resolved early to make life easier for her. She took various jobs—seamstress, companion, governess and teacher—to support the family. But it was at her writing table that she was most successful. While she was in her twenties, a variety of thrillers, poems, potboilers and "sensation stories" poured forth from her pen under other names.

In 1868, her Boston publisher suggested that she write a novel for girls using scenes and people familiar to her. So, with her family's encouragement, she wrote *Little Women,* which originally appeared in two volumes.

She was able to write the book very quickly—for she had prepared for thirty-five years, and her cast of characters was her own family!

The story was an immediate and huge success. The publisher could not print copies fast enough to keep the orders filled. The demand for more of Louisa's stories was so great that she followed up with a book nearly every year till the end of her life. Among them are *Little Men, Eight Cousins, Jo's Boys* and *Under the Lilacs.*

Louisa was a great champion of causes, such as better working conditions for women and women's suffrage. She was the first woman in Concord to register to vote.

Louisa became very famous, and though life was comfortable, she felt her freedom restricted because of her fame. Her success brought her little happiness, and she died, nervous and exhausted, at the age of fifty-six.

Characters You Will Meet

The March Sisters
Meg
Jo
Beth
Amy
Marmee, *their mother*
Mr. March, *their father*
Hannah, *the servant*
Theodore Laurence, called Laurie, *their neighbor*
Mr. Laurence, *his grandfather*
Aunt March, *Mr. March's aunt*
John Brooke, *Laurie's tutor*
Esther, *Aunt March's maid*
Aunt Carrol, *another of the March's aunts*
Mrs. Kirke, *a friend of Mrs. March in New York*
Mr. Friedrich Bhaer, *a boarder at Mrs. Kirke's house*

The March Sisters

Chapter 1
Four Sisters

The four March sisters sat around the fire knitting while they waited for their mother to come home.

"Christmas won't be Christmas without any presents," grumbled Jo.

"It's so dreadful to be poor," sighed Meg.

"Some girls have all the pretty things, while others have nothing," sniffed Amy.

"But we've got Mother and Father and each other," said Beth from her corner.

"But we haven't got Father. We shall not have him for a long time," said Jo. Father was off where the fighting was. Though too old to fight, he had gone as a chaplain.

Each girl had a dollar to spend on something she wanted for Christmas. But there were to be no presents this year. Mother thought they should not spend money on pleasure when the men were suffering in the dreadful American Civil War.

Although they were poor, they were a happy and close family. The room in which they sat was comfortable and warm, though the furniture was plain.

Margaret, or Meg, was the oldest of the four at sixteen. She was pretty, with soft brown hair. Fifteen-year-old Jo was tall and thin, and something of a tomboy. Her one beauty was her long, thick hair. Beth, who was thirteen, was very shy. She had a timid voice, and she seldom left the house. Amy, though the youngest, felt herself to be very important. She had big blue eyes and curly

Father Is a Chaplain.

golden hair.

The clock struck six and reminded them that Marmee, as they called their mother, would soon be home. Suddenly they all had the same idea. They would each buy something for Marmee with their dollars.

"We must go shopping tomorrow, Meg," said Jo, marching up and down. They were all excitedly planning when Marmee, a tall, motherly lady opened the door. She was not elegantly dressed, but they thought her noble-looking. The girls helped her get her wet things off and get settled by the fire.

"I've got a treat for you after supper," said Mrs. March. "A letter from Father! A nice long letter. He is well and sends loving wishes for Christmas."

"Oh, when will he come home, Mother?" asked Beth with a quiver in her voice.

"Not for many months, unless he is sick. He will stay and do his work," said Mrs.

Getting Marmee Settled

March sadly.

They all drew to the fire to hear the letter. It was cheerful and full of news, but everyone sniffed when they came to the end. Father said he would not be back for a year. Everyone was quiet, and then they again fell to their work.

At nine they stopped work and sang before they went to bed. Beth, the musical one, played the old piano. Meg and Marmee led the singing while Jo gave a croak or two in the wrong place, and Amy chirped like a cricket. Then they all went up to bed.

The Evening Sing

"Where Is Mother?"

Chapter 2
A Merry Christmas

Jo was the first to wake on Christmas morning. No stockings hung at the fireplace. But she reached under her pillow and found a small crimson-covered book. She woke Meg, who received a green-covered book. The two younger girls each received books too.

"Where is Mother?" asked Meg as she and Jo ran downstairs. Hannah, the servant who had been with the family since Meg was born, answered that a boy had come begging and Mrs. March had gone with him to see what his family needed.

"She'll be back soon, so let's have everything ready," said Meg. The gifts were collected in a basket and put under the sofa. There were new slippers from Jo, gloves from Meg, embroidered handkerchiefs from Beth, and a bottle of perfume from Amy.

The door banged and Mrs. March entered. "Merry Christmas, Marmee!" the girls cried together.

"Merry Christmas, daughters. I want to say one word before we sit down. Not far away from here is a woman named Mrs. Hummel and her baby and six children. They are suffering from hunger and cold. Will you give them your breakfast as a Christmas gift?"

They were all hungry, but they said yes and soon set out to bring the poor Hummel family a Christmas breakfast.

When they arrived, they built a fire with the wood they brought and spread the food on the table for the grateful children.

A Christmas Present from the Marches

When they returned home, they presented their mother with the gifts. Mrs. March was surprised and touched, and there was a good deal of laughing and hugging.

The rest of the day was devoted to preparations for the evening. When the girls went down to supper, they stared at the table in amazement. There was ice cream and cake and fruit and in the middle of the table, huge bouquets of fresh flowers.

Mrs. March said that Mr. Laurence, their neighbor, had sent all the goodies.

"The Laurence boy's grandfather! Why, we don't even know him," exclaimed Meg.

"Well," Mrs. March said, "he heard about your breakfast party and sent over a few trifles in honor of the day."

"The boy put it into his head. I know he did!" cried Jo. "He's such a good fellow, I wish we could get to know him."

Mr. Laurence and his grandson lived next

The Marches' Christmas Table

door, but the March girls hardly knew the boy. Everyone said the grandfather kept the boy inside with his tutor, Mr. Brooke, and made him study all the time.

"When the cat ran away, he brought her back," said Jo. "And I've talked with him over the fence. I want to get to know him. I think he needs some fun."

They talked about it while they ate the ice, and everyone agreed they had never seen such beautiful flowers.

Jo Thinks About the Laurence Boy.

"What Shall We Wear?"

Chapter 3
The Laurence Boy

"Jo, where are you?" cried Meg. "We have just received an invitation to a little holiday dance. Marmee said we may go, but what *shall* we wear?"

"We shall wear our cotton dresses, for they're the only ones we've got," answered Jo practically. "Yours is fine, but mine is burned in the back."

"You must sit still then and keep your back out of sight," said Meg. "And you must behave. I'll give you a signal if I see you doing anything wrong."

The next night the two younger sisters helped the older girls get ready for the party. There was much running up and down, laughing and talking. Finally they were ready. Meg's high heeled slippers were very tight and hurt her. Jo said the hairpins were sticking into her head.

When they arrived at the party, they joined a group of girls, but Jo didn't care much for girls or gossip, so she wandered off. No one came to talk to her, and she couldn't move around because her burned dress would show.

She finally slipped into a corner that was curtained off and was surprised to see that another bashful person was already there. It was "the Laurence boy."

"Dear me, I didn't know anybody was in here," stammered Jo.

But the boy laughed and said pleasantly, "Don't mind me. Stay if you like."

"You live near us, don't you, Mr. Laurence?"

The Laurence Boy

said Jo, trying to be polite.

"Next door," the boy said. "But I'm not Mr. Laurence, I'm only Laurie. My first name is Theodore, but I like Laurie better."

They were soon talking and laughing. Laurie felt at ease with Jo, and Jo liked "the Laurence boy" better than ever. She looked at him carefully. He was fifteen years old, and he had curly black hair, big black eyes, and a handsome nose.

Soon Meg beckoned to her sister, and Jo reluctantly followed her into a side room. Meg was holding her foot. "I've sprained my ankle. That stupid high heel turned, and I can hardly stand. How am I ever going to get home?"

"I'll ask Laurie. He'll go for a carriage," said Jo.

"Mercy no!" said Meg. "Don't ask or tell anyone." Jo then went off to get Meg some supper and ended up spilling coffee on her

"I've Sprained My Ankle!"

dress.

She heard a friendly voice behind her say, "Can I help you?" It was Laurie. Jo explained that she was bringing supper to Meg, who had hurt herself. Laurie was very helpful. He offered his grandfather's carriage to take the girls home, saying it was no trouble. When it was time to go, he rode up in front, so the sisters could talk over their adventures.

The morning after the party, everyone was out of sorts. Meg complained and Jo grumbled as they left the house. But the sight of their mother waving and smiling in the window when they turned back made them feel more cheerful.

When Mr. March lost his property in trying to help an unfortunate friend, the two older girls offered to go to work to help the family. Meg found a place as a nursery governess. But she was more fond of luxury than the others and found the family's poverty especially hard to bear.

Meg and Jo Leave for Work.

Something about Jo struck old Aunt March, who was lame and needed a companion. Taking care of a peppery old lady did not suit Jo at all, but she could not refuse. The real attraction about going to Aunt March's was her large library of fine books. The moment Aunt March took her nap or was busy with company, Jo hurried to this quiet place.

Jo wanted to do something splendid with her life, but meanwhile, she loved to read and be boyish. Her quick temper, sharp tongue and restless spirit were always getting her into trouble.

Beth was too bashful to go to school. She had tried it, but she suffered so much that now she did her lessons at home. She was a homey little creature and helped Hannah. Beth would weep every once in a while because she couldn't take music lessons or have a fine piano, but no one ever saw her.

If anybody had asked Amy what the

Jo Loved Aunt March's Library.

greatest trial of her life was, she would have answered, "My nose." She pinched and pulled it, but it always remained rather flat. Amy had a talent for drawing, and her teachers complained that she covered her slate and books with pictures. She was a great favorite with everyone and was well on her way to being spoiled, even though she had to wear her cousin's hand-me-down dresses.

Amy confided in Meg, and Meg took special care of her. By some strange attraction of opposites, Jo and Beth were drawn to each other. The two older girls loved one another very much, but each took one of the younger girls into her keeping and watched over her in her own way.

The Greatest Trial of Amy's Life

Jo Sees Laurie at the Window.

Chapter 4
Being Neighborly

A garden with a low hedge separated the March's house from Mr. Laurence's house. The Laurence house was a stately stone mansion, with a big coach house and well-kept grounds. Yet it seemed a lonely house, and few people went in and out except the old gentleman and his grandson.

Jo longed to go inside and get to know "the Laurence boy," who looked as if he'd like to be known. One day she spied his wistful face at an upper window.

"There he is," thought Jo, "poor boy! All

alone! He needs someone to play with!" So when she went out, she tossed a snowball up to the window and called out, "How do you do? Wouldn't you like some nice girl to come over and amuse you?"

"I don't know any," he answered.

"You know us," said Jo and laughed.

"So I do. Will you come please?" cried Laurie.

Presently Jo appeared with a covered dish. "Mother sent her love and wanted me to bring you some custard. It isn't anything, but everyone felt kindly and wanted to show it."

They sat down in Laurie's parlor to talk. "I'll talk all day if I get going," said Jo. "Beth says I never know when to stop."

Laurie knew who each of the girls was, which surprised Jo. "I often hear you calling to one another," he explained, "and when I'm alone, I can't help looking over at your house. I haven't any mother, you know," he added

Jo Comes to Visit.

sadly.

"I just wish you'd come over. We'd have such jolly times," she said. "Wouldn't your grandpa let you? We're not strangers, we're neighbors."

They talked on and on, and then Laurie asked Jo to come see the house and his grandpa's books. He led her from room to room. "What riches!" sighed Jo when they reached the library. She stood before a fine portrait of the old gentleman and never heard the door open.

"What have you been doing to this boy of mine?" said the gruff voice of Mr. Laurence. Poor Jo couldn't blush any redder. Although his voice was gruff, the gentleman's eyes twinkled.

"Only trying to be neighborly, sir," she said. "Laurie seems a little lonely."

"So he is, but tea is about to be served, so come down and go on being neighborly."

"What Have You Been Doing to My Boy?"

The old gentleman did not say much as he drank his tea, but he watched the young people chatting away like old friends. He liked Jo, for her odd blunt ways suited him. And before she left, Laurie took her to the drawing room and played the grand piano while Jo listened.

When Jo got home and related her afternoon's adventures, Mrs. March said "her friend" was very welcome at the March house.

All sorts of nice things started to happen. Everyone liked Laurie, and what good times they had! Meg walked in the Laurence's conservatory, Jo browsed in the library, and Amy copied pictures.

But Beth could not pluck up courage to go to the "mansion" and play the grand piano. She was afraid of gruff Mr. Laurence, but when he heard about this, he set to mending matters.

Laurie Plays the Grand Piano.

He sat in the March's parlor and led the conversation to music. "Wouldn't some of you girls like to run over and practice on the piano, just to keep it in tune? You needn't say anything to anybody, but run in at any time."

This was too much of a temptation for Beth. Next day, after two or three tries, she went in the side door and made her way noiselessly to the drawing room to play. She stayed until dinnertime and then could only sit and smile at everyone. After that, she slipped through the hedge nearly every day.

A few weeks later, she decided to make Mr. Laurence a pair of slippers to show her special thanks. She wrote a simple note and, with Laurie's help, got them smuggled into the old gentleman's study.

The next day passed, and the next, and Beth went out to do an errand. When she came back, her sisters led her to the parlor.

Beth Enters the Drawing Room.

There stood a little piano, with a letter addressed to Miss Elizabeth March.

"For me?" gasped Beth, holding onto Jo.

"Yes, all for you. Don't you think he's the dearest old man in the world? Try it. Let's hear the sound of the piano."

So Beth tried it, and everyone said it was the most remarkable piano they ever heard.

"You'll have to go and thank him," said Jo, though she didn't think Beth would ever go.

"Yes, I guess I'll go now, before I get frightened thinking about it." And to the family's amazement, Beth walked through the hedge and into the Laurence's door.

Beth knocked at the study door and with a trembling voice said, "I came to thank you, sir, for—" but she forgot her speech and put her arms round his neck. And from that moment she stopped fearing the gruff Mr. Laurence.

Beth Thanks Mr. Laurence.

Amy Wants to Go Too.

Chapter 5
Jo and Her Temper

"Girls, where are you going?" asked Amy, finding Jo and Meg getting ready to go out.

"Never mind. Little girls shouldn't ask questions," returned Jo.

"I know!" said Amy. "You're going to the theatre with Laurie! Oh, please, let me come too!"

"If she goes, I won't. Laurie only invited us," said Jo crossly. Amy wailed, which made Jo even more cross.

Just as they were setting out, Amy called down the stairs in a threatening tone, "You'll be sorry for this, Jo March! See if you're not!"

They had a splendid time, although several times Jo thought of her quick temper and how she tried to control it.

When they got home, they found Amy reading in the parlor. Jo took a quick look around her room, but everything seemed to be in place.

There Jo was mistaken, for the next day, she discovered that her writing book had disappeared.

"Amy, you've got it," she said.

"No, I haven't."

"You know where it is then," cried Jo, giving her a shake. "You'd better tell or I'll make you!"

"You'll never get it back," cried Amy, getting very excited. "I burned it up!"

"What! My book with all my writing in it?" said Jo, turning pale.

"Yes, I told you I'd make you pay—" Amy

Jo Gives Amy a Shake.

got no further for Jo shook her until her teeth chattered, crying:

"You wicked, wicked girl! I'll never forgive you as long as I live," and she rushed out of the room.

Jo's book was the pride of her heart, and she had worked over all the stories in it carefully. Amy's bonfire had burned up several years of work.

When the bell rang for tea, Jo appeared and Amy asked for forgiveness. "I shall never forgive you" was Jo's stern reply, and she said nothing more all evening.

Nothing went well the next day either, so Jo decided to ask Laurie to go skating. "He is always kind and jolly and will make me happier," she thought, and off she went.

Amy heard the sound of skates and, wanting to go very badly, decided to follow. It was not far to the river, but both Laurie and Jo had their skates on before Amy reached

Laurie and Jo Had Their Skates On.

them. Jo saw her and turned her back. Laurie went on ahead, testing the ice, for the weather had been warm. As he turned the bend, he shouted back, "Keep near the shore. It isn't safe in the middle."

Jo heard, but Amy was struggling to her feet and didn't hear a word.

Laurie was way ahead, Jo was just at the turn, and Amy was skating toward the middle. There was a strange feeling in Jo's heart, and something made her turn just in time to see Amy throw up her hands and crash through the soft ice. She tried to yell for Laurie; she tried to rush forward.

Laurie was by her in a flash, calling, "Bring a rail, quick!"

How she did it she didn't know. But while Laurie, lying flat, held Amy up by his arm, she got a rail from the fence and together they got her out.

Amy, shivering, dripping and crying, was

Amy Crashes Through the Ice.

bundled in Laurie's coat and rushed home. In no time, she was asleep before the warm fire.

Jo had hardly spoken. She looked pale and wild, and later dropped at her mother's side. "It's my dreadful temper," she cried. "If she had died, it would have been my fault."

"Well, you have learned a lesson," said her mother. "My temper used to be worse than yours, but I have learned to check it. I am angry nearly every day, but I do not show it. Your father has helped me."

It made them both sad to think of Father, and they held each other. Then Jo hugged Amy, who stirred in her sleep and hugged her back.

Jo Blames Her Dreadful Temper.

Helping Meg Pack Her Trunk

Chapter 6
Meg Tries to Be Fashionable

In April, Meg's friend, Annie Moffat, invited her for a two-week stay. The Moffats were very fashionable, and Mrs. March was afraid Meg's head would be turned.

The other girls helped her pack her trunk. There were going to be several small parties and a large party on Thursday. In went her old and mended white cotton party dress, along with her other everyday dresses and her old bonnet.

After Meg was at the Moffat's a few days, she began to imitate those around her and put on airs. The more she saw Annie Moffat's things, the more she envied her and sighed to be rich.

When the evening for one of the small parties came, out came Meg's old "ball dress," looking shabbier than ever. Meg saw the girls glance at it and then at one another, and her cheeks began to burn.

Then the maid came in with a box of flowers for Meg, and the girls gathered around, wanting to know who they were from.

"The note is from Mother, and the flowers are from Laurie," Meg said. Annie gave her sister a funny look. "He often sends us flowers; my mother and old Mr. Laurence are friends, you know." Meg felt almost happy again and enjoyed herself very much that evening. She didn't know why, but the next day the Moffat girls seemed to treat her with more interest and respect. They told her they'd sent an invitation to the young Mr. Laurence for Thursday's party.

Meg laughed, saying, "Laurie is only a little boy." Again the sisters exchanged looks.

Flowers for Meg

Annie's sister offered Meg her blue silk dress for Thursday's party, and on Thursday evening they made Meg into a fine lady. They laced her into the dress, which was very tight, crimped her hair, and gave her earrings and high heeled boots.

"I'm afraid to go down, I feel so stiff and half dressed," said Meg to Annie. But she acted the part of a fine lady though the tight dress gave her a side ache and she kept tripping over the train.

She was flirting and laughing when she saw Laurie staring at her with surprise. "I'm glad you came," she said to him in her most grown-up way.

"Jo wanted me to come and tell her how you looked," replied Laurie.

"Well, wouldn't Jo stare if she saw me? Do you like me dressed up like this?"

"No, I don't" was his blunt reply.

That was altogether too much from a lad

Meg Flirts at the Party.

younger than she. Meg walked away and stood by a window, where she overheard a gentleman saying, "They are making a fool of that little girl, dressing her like a doll."

"Oh dear," thought Meg, "I should have worn my own things."

"Laurie," she whispered when he asked her to dance, "please do me a favor and don't tell them at home about my dress. I'd rather tell them myself how silly I've been. I feel horrid. I only wanted a little fun, but I've found this doesn't pay."

Laurie agreed, but he was not pleased at the change he saw in her.

Meg was sick from too much champagne all the next day and found that she had not enjoyed herself as much as she expected. On Saturday she went home, and home seemed like a very nice place, even if it wasn't splendid.

Meg told her adventures to everyone. She

Meg Admits She Has Been Silly.

confessed later to Jo and her mother that she had allowed the Moffat girls to dress her up, and that she had romped and flirted after drinking too much champagne.

She also told them bits of gossip, especially one part she'd overheard about Mrs. March having "plans" for Laurie and her daughters because he was rich.

Jo said it was all rubbish, and Mrs. March ended by telling what her plans were:

"I want my daughters to be admired, loved and respected; to be well and to lead useful lives; and to marry only for love and happiness."

Meg Tells About the Gossip.

Beth, the Postmistress

Chapter 7
Summer and Dreams

Spring came, and gardening, walks, rowing on the river, and flower hunts filled the lengthening days.

To promote friendly relations between households, Laurie set up a post office made out of an old bird house in the hedge between the two houses.

The post office was very well used by everyone, even Mr. Laurence. Beth was postmistress. She was always home, and she liked the job of distributing the mail.

One day, Jo got an invitation from Laurie

to a picnic at Longmeadow with some of his English friends and Mr. Brooke, his tutor. The girls were invited for lunch and croquet.

Meg thought her dress of printed cotton would be just the thing. Beth said she would come if Jo promised not to let any of the boys talk to her. "I like to please Laurie," she added, "and I'm not afraid of Mr. Brooke. I'll work hard and not trouble anyone."

The sun shone brightly the next morning, and all the girls were making their own preparations. Amy had slept all night with a clothespin on her nose to try to give it a little uplift. Beth kept reporting what was going on next door. She saw the carriage full of people arrive and urged the girls to hurry.

"Oh, Jo, you're not going to wear that awful hat," said Meg as they were leaving.

"I just will," said Jo. "I don't mind being a boy, and this hat is fun." And with that, Jo marched off followed by the others.

Off for the Picnic at Longmeadow

Laurie ran to meet them and presented his friends. The party was soon ready to board the two boats.

Mr. Brooke and Ned Moffat rowed one boat, and Laurie and Jo rowed the other. The two friends were always together and shared a special friendship. Jo had a pet name for Laurie, which only she used. She called him Teddy.

Jo's funny hat produced a laugh from all, but Kate, the oldest of Laurie's English guests, looked amazed at everything Jo did.

Meg, in the other boat, faced Mr. Brooke, Laurie's tutor. He was a grave, silent young man, with handsome brown eyes and a pleasant voice. Meg liked his quiet manners and considered him to have a great store of useful knowledge. He never talked to her much, but he looked at her a great deal.

It was not far to Longmeadow. As they landed, Laurie suggested a game of croquet.

Meg Faces Mr. Brooke.

They then had lunch, and a very merry one it was. Cups and plates were overturned, acorns dropped into the milk, and little ants and caterpillars attended.

When lunch was over, Kate, Meg and Mr. Brooke—the older people—sat apart. Kate had a sketch pad and Mr. Brooke lay on the grass with a book.

Kate asked Meg if she went to school, and Meg replied, "No, I'm a governess."

"Oh, indeed," Kate said, but she might as well have said, "How dreadful!"

Mr. Brooke looked up and said quickly, "Young ladies in America are very independent. They are admired and respected for supporting themselves."

"Oh, yes, of course," said Kate, getting up. "How odd these Americans are," she thought. "I hope Laurie won't be spoiled among them."

"I forgot that English people turn up their noses at governesses and don't treat them as

Meg Is Annoyed.

we do," said Meg with an annoyed expression when Kate walked away.

"Tutors also have a hard time of it there," said Mr. Brooke, smiling. "But I shan't be a tutor for long. Laurie goes to college next year and when he goes, I will join the army."

"Laurie and his grandfather and all of us will be very sorry to see you go," said Meg, but she could not help noticing the way he looked at her.

One day, when the vacation was nearly over, Laurie said to the girls, "I have so many dreams, it would be hard to choose the one I'd want. But I'll tell my favorite one if you all will tell yours."

They agreed. So Laurie began:

"I'd like to see the world and then settle in Germany and be a famous musician."

Meg seemed to find it hard to tell hers, but she said, "I want a lovely house full of luxurious things and heaps of money."

Sharing Favorite Dreams

"You know your castle wouldn't be perfect without a good husband and some children," said Jo.

"You'd have nothing but inkstands and novels in yours," said Meg.

"Wouldn't I, though!" said Jo. "I want to do something special. I think I shall write books and get famous. That would suit me."

"My favorite dream is to stay home and take care of the family," said Beth. "Since I have my piano, I am satisfied."

"I want to be an artist and go to Rome and do fine pictures," said Amy.

Laurie was going to college in a few weeks. It was to please his grandfather, but he said he sometimes felt like breaking away and pleasing himself.

Jo, who was always ready with a plan, said, "If we are all alive in ten years, let's meet and see how many of us have got our wishes." And they all agreed.

Planning a Meeting in Ten Years

Jo Takes Her Manuscripts to the City.

Chapter 8
Secrets

When the fall came, Jo was busy in the garret, her special hideaway where she did all her writing. When she finished her manuscript, she took it and another one from the drawer, and crept down and out the door.

She went at a fast pace to the city and stood by a certain door, then gave herself a shake and went in. In ten minutes she came out looking as if she'd had a trying ordeal. Laurie was waiting for her. He had seen her leave in a determined manner and decided to follow.

"Why are you here alone? Are you up to some mischief, Jo?" said Laurie. "I have a secret to tell, but if I do, you must tell me why you're here."

"Well, Teddy, if you won't say anything at home or tease me, I'll tell," said Jo. "I've left two stories with a newspaperman, and he's going to tell me if he likes them next week."

"Hurrah for Miss March, the celebrated author!" shouted Laurie.

"Hush, it may not come to anything. But I had to try. Now tell me your secret."

"Brooke has Meg's glove," whispered Laurie. "Isn't it romantic?"

Jo looked displeased. "I wish you hadn't told me. I don't like the idea of anyone coming to take Meg away." Lately Jo had felt that Meg was getting to be a woman, and she dreaded the separation she knew was soon to come.

For the next two weeks, Jo behaved very strangely. She rushed to the door when the postman rang, was rude to Mr. Brooke, and whispered a lot to Laurie. Two Saturdays

Telling Secrets

later, Meg heard shrieks of laughter and a great flapping of newspapers from Jo and Laurie in the yard.

"What shall we do with that girl? She never will behave like a young lady," said Meg. In a few minutes Jo bounced in and offered to read a story from the paper. Everyone listened with interest, and then Jo couldn't resist announcing she had written it!

"You?" cried Meg.

"I knew it! I knew it! Oh, Jo, I'm so proud." Beth ran to hug her sister.

Then Jo told them to stop jabbering so she could tell the whole story. When her breath gave out, she wrapped her head in the paper and cried a few tears on it.

Jo's Story in the Newspaper!

Bad News

Chapter 9
A Telegram

November came, and the girls said it was the most disagreeable month in the year.

Meg sat at the table when Mrs. March came in with her usual, "Any letter from Father, girls? It's our day for a letter."

There was a sharp ring at the door, and Hannah came in with a telegram. Mrs. March snatched it, read it, and dropped back into her chair. Jo read aloud in a frightened voice:

"MRS. MARCH:

YOUR HUSBAND IS VERY ILL. COME AT ONCE TO WASHINGTON."

How still the room was. The whole world suddenly seemed to change. Mrs. March was herself again in a minute and said, "I shall go at once, but it may be too late."

First there was the sound of sobbing, but then everyone set about to help Mrs. March get ready. Laurie was to go send a telegram and drop off a note at Aunt March's. The money for the sad trip would have to be borrowed. It was decided that Mr. Brooke would go too. Everything was arranged by the time Laurie returned. But where was Jo? They began to worry when she burst in and laid a roll of bills before her mother.

"That's for making Father comfortable and bringing him home. I earned it. I only sold what was my own."

As she spoke, she took off her bonnet, and everyone saw that all her beautiful hair—the hair she was so proud of—was cut off and sold. They all exclaimed and Beth went to hug her.

Jo's Beautiful Hair Is Gone!

"What made you do it?" asked Amy, who would as soon have cut off her head as her pretty hair.

"I wanted to do something for Father. As I was passing a barber's window, I saw some hair pieces in there, and I knew I had one thing to make money out of. So I walked in and asked if he bought hair.

"The barber was not used to having girls bounce in his shop offering to sell their hair, but I begged him to take it."

Mrs. March thanked her, and they tried to talk of other things. No one wanted to go to bed that night. Beth went to the piano and played Father's favorite hymn.

Meg lay awake for hours when all of a sudden she heard a stifled sob. "My hair," Jo cried into her pillow. "It's vain and selfish, but I can't help it. It was my one beauty."

They had breakfast in the cold gray dawn. The trunk was ready in the hall. Nobody

The Barber Cut Jo's Hair.

talked much, but as they sat waiting for the carriage, Mrs. March said:

"Girls, I leave you to Hannah's care and Mr. Laurence's protection. Go on with your work as usual. Hope and keep busy. Meg, watch over your sisters. Be patient, Jo, and don't do rash things. Beth, comfort yourself with your music, and Amy, help all you can."

There was one hard minute. They kissed their mother and tried to wave cheerfully when she drove away.

News from their father comforted the girls. He was dangerously ill, but Mrs. March had already done him good. Mr. Brooke sent a bulletin every day, and they became more cheerful as the weeks passed.

Everyone was eager to write, and plump letters full of news and cheer were sent to Washington by the sisters.

A Hard Good-Bye

Beth Slips Out Alone.

Chapter 10
Dark Days

For a week after their mother left, the girls were as helpful as they could be. Beth kept on, doing her own duties and many of her sisters' too.

Ten days after Mrs. March's departure, Beth tried to get one of her sisters to go with her to visit poor families, as their mother had done. "The Hummel baby is sick," she said, "and I don't know what to do for it."

Jo was reading a story, Meg went upstairs, and Amy did not come, so Beth silently slipped out into the chilly air.

When Jo went upstairs later, she found

Beth looking very grave and ill.

"What's the matter?" cried Jo.

"Oh, Jo, Mrs. Hummel's baby died on my lap while I was holding it. Scarlet fever!"

"How dreadful! I ought to have gone," said Jo taking her sister in her arms. "Oh, Beth, if you should be sick, I never could forgive myself."

"Don't be frightened," said Beth, whose cheeks were flushed and forehead hot. "I shan't have it badly. I did take some medicine, and I feel better."

"I'll call Hannah," said Jo. "She'll know what to do."

Hannah came and assured Jo there was no need to worry. Everyone had scarlet fever. If treated right, no one died.

"We'll call Dr. Bangs and send Amy off to Aunt March's so she won't catch it. You and Meg can stay at home."

When Amy was told, she cried and then

Scarlet Fever!

declared she'd rather have the fever than go to Aunt March. She became agreeable only when Laurie promised to come and take her for a ride every day.

Dr. Bangs said that Beth did have symptoms of fever. They decided not to tell Mrs. March, as she couldn't leave Father, and it would only make her worry.

Beth was much sicker than anyone but Hannah and the doctor suspected. She would wake and then sink back into the fever fits. She did not even recognize the familiar faces around her.

Still Mrs. March was not told. Jo devoted herself to Beth night and day. Laurie haunted the house like a ghost.

The first of December was a wintry day. When Dr. Bangs came that morning, he looked at Beth and said, "If Mrs. March can leave her husband, she'd better be sent for."

Jo snatched up a telegram and rushed out.

"Mrs. March Must Be Sent For."

"I've sent for Mother," she said to Laurie when she returned. "The doctor told us to."

"Oh, Jo, it's not so bad as that?" cried Laurie.

The tears started to stream down Jo's cheeks. Laurie held out his hand and whispered, "I'm here. Hold on to me, Jo dear. Keep hoping for the best. Your mother will be here soon, and everything will be all right. I telegraphed her yesterday, and she'll be here tonight." Soon Jo dried her eyes. Laurie beamed. "Aren't you glad I did it?"

Jo threw her arms around his neck, and Laurie patted her back. He even followed it up with a bashful kiss or two.

"I got Grandpa to say it was time we did something. The late train comes in at 2:00 A.M. I shall go for her."

A breath of fresh air seemed to blow through the house. Everyone rejoiced but Beth. All day long Meg and Jo hovered over

Laurie Comforts Jo.

her. The hours dragged by. The doctor came and said some change would take place about midnight.

The girls did not sleep that night. The clock struck twelve. An hour went by. Nothing happened except Laurie's departure for the station.

At two o'clock it looked to Jo as if a change had taken place, so she woke Hannah, who ran to Beth and exclaimed, "The fever has broken. She's sleeping naturally. Praise be given!"

Both girls crept into the dark hall and held each other close. "If Mother would only come," said Jo, as the sky started to lighten.

Then there was the sound of bells at the door below and Laurie's voice crying, "Girls, she's come! Marmee's come!"

The Fever Has Broken!

A Hard Time at Aunt March's

Chapter 11
Serious Conversations

While these things were happening at home, Amy was having a hard time at Aunt March's. Aunt March took Amy in hand to teach her the way she had been taught sixty years ago.

Amy had to do all of Aunt's tiresome labors and read aloud after dinner. If it had not been for Laurie and old Esther, the maid, she felt she could not have gotten through. Esther took a fancy to Amy and let her examine all the curious and pretty things stored away in the big house. Amy's chief delight was a big cabinet full of jewelry. "I wish I knew where all these pretty things will go when Aunt March dies," Amy said to Esther, replacing the jewels.

"To you and your sisters. I have seen Madame's will," whispered Esther.

"How nice! But I wish she'd let us have them now," said Amy.

"It is too soon. But that little turquoise ring will be given to you when you go home, for Madame approves of you."

"Do you think so? I'll be very good if only I can have that ring. I do like Aunt March, after all," added Amy.

From that day on, she was a model of obedience, and the old lady thought her training was very successful.

But when Laurie came and said that Beth was in danger, Amy went and prayed for her, feeling that a million turquoise rings would not make up for losing her gentle sister.

Amy Wants the Turquoise Ring.

With Mother home, the house was full of genuine happiness. Beth woke from her sleep, and her eyes fell on her mother. Then she slept again, and Meg and Jo waited on their mother. They heard all the news of Father and Mr. Brooke, and then they closed their weary eyes to sleep. Mrs. March wouldn't leave Beth's side and rested in the big chair.

Laurie went off to keep Amy posted. But he fell asleep on the sofa after his long night and was awakened by Amy's cry of joy at the sight of her mother.

As Amy was talking, Mrs. March saw the ring on her hand. Amy said, "Aunt March gave me the ring today, and I'd like to wear it to remind me not to be selfish. Beth isn't selfish and that's why everyone loves her."

"Wear your ring, dear, and do your best," said Mrs. March. "Now I must get back to Beth."

That evening, Jo found her mother in

Amy Runs to Her Mother.

Beth's room and said, "I want to talk to you, Mother."

"About Meg?" questioned Mrs. March.

"Yes. How did you know? Mr. Brooke has one of Meg's gloves, and Teddy saw it and teased him. He said he liked Meg but didn't dare say anything because she was so young and he was so poor. I don't know anything about love and such nonsense!" cried Jo.

"Dear, don't get angry. John—that's what we call Mr. Brooke now—went with me and was very devoted to Father. He was very open about his love for Meg. He told us he wanted to marry her. He is an excellent young man, but I will not consent to Meg's marrying so young."

"Of course not! It would be idiotic. It's worse than I imagined!" cried Jo.

"Don't say anything to Meg," said Mrs. March. "I don't know whether she loves John yet. But I'll be able to judge better when I see

Jo Tells Marmee about Mr. Brooke.

them together."

"I see it all! When he comes back, it will all be settled. He will marry her and take her off and make a hole in our family," moaned Jo.

"Meg is only seventeen," said Mrs. March. "Your father and I have agreed that Meg shall not marry before she is twenty. If she and John love each other, they can wait."

Just then Meg entered the room with a letter she was writing to Father, and Mrs. March said, "Please add that I send my love to John."

"Do you call him 'John'?" asked Meg, smiling.

"Yes, he has been like a son to us," replied Mrs. March, looking at her daughter.

Meg only smiled and said, "Good night, Mother dear. It is so comfortable to have you home."

A Letter for Father

A Christmas Snow Maiden for Beth

Chapter 12
Aunt March Settles the Question

As Christmas neared, both invalids improved. Mr. March wrote that he would soon be home with them, and Beth was brought downstairs to lie on the sofa all day.

On Christmas morning, Beth was carried to the window to see the stately snow maiden Jo and Laurie had made during the night. Laurie ran up and down bringing in the gifts.

"I'm so full of happiness that if Father were here, I couldn't hold one drop more," said Beth.

Half an hour later, Laurie opened the parlor door and in a breathless voice said,

"Here's another present for the Marches."

There in the doorway was a tall man, leaning on the arm of another tall man. For several minutes everybody seemed to lose their wits. Then they ran to embrace Mr. March. Jo nearly fainted and had to be tended to by Laurie. Mr. Brooke kissed Meg entirely by mistake. Amy sobbed on her father's boots.

Then the study door flew open, and Beth ran straight into her father's arms.

Mr. March told them how he had wanted to surprise them, and when the fine weather came, he and Mr. Brooke took advantage of it to return home.

There was a gay Christmas dinner that night with the family, Mr. Laurence and his grandson, and Mr. Brooke. After dinner, the family sat around the fire.

"Just a year ago we were groaning, remember?" asked Jo.

"It's been a rather rough road for you to

Another Present for the Marches

travel," said Mr. March, looking at the four faces, "but you have got on bravely." Mr. March then praised each of them—Meg for her hard work, Jo for how ladylike and gentle she had become, Beth for not being as shy as she used to be, and Amy for thinking of other people more and herself less.

Then, for the first time in many months, Beth went slowly to her place at the little piano for the evening song.

The next day, there was a strange feeling in the house. Meg was absent-minded, shy and silent, and blushed when John's name was mentioned.

She told Jo that she would act very calm if Mr. Brooke did propose. But a tap on the door made her lose her dignity entirely, and she started sewing furiously.

It *was* Mr. Brooke, and Jo slipped out of the room. Meg rose to go and started to murmur, but Mr. Brooke took her hand.

Meg Tries to Act Calm.

"Oh, please don't go, Meg. I won't trouble you, I only want to know if you care for me a little. I love you so."

This was the moment for the calm proper speech, but Meg just hung her head and answered, "I don't know." John begged and Meg faltered. He was grave and pale, but tender.

It was at this moment that Aunt March hobbled into the room. She had heard Mr. March was home and had rushed over.

"Bless me, what's this?" cried the old lady as Mr. Brooke left the room.

"It's Father's friend," stammered Meg. "I'm so surprised to see you."

"There's mischief going on and I want to know what it is. Tell me, do you mean to marry this man? If you do, not one penny of my money ever goes to you!"

"I'll marry whom I please, Aunt March," said Meg, raising her chin.

"Highty-tighty! Is that the way you take

Aunt March Enters.

my advice? It's your duty to marry well and help your family. But I see you intend to marry a man without money, position or business. I thought you had more sense."

"We are willing to work, and we mean to wait. I'm not afraid of being poor. I know I shall be happy because he loves me."

Aunt March was very angry. She had counted on making a good match for pretty Meg. "Well, I wash my hands of the whole affair. I'm disappointed in you and haven't the heart to see your father now. Don't expect anything from me when you're married."

She slammed the door in Meg's face and drove off. Mr. Brooke came running in.

"I couldn't help hearing, Meg. It proves that you do care for me a little bit."

Fifteen minutes after Aunt March's departure, Jo came softly downstairs and stopped dead at the scene she saw. Meg was sitting on John's knee, looking blissful. Jo gasped,

Aunt March Is Very Angry.

and John said, "Sister Jo, congratulate us!"

This was too much! Jo ran upstairs and told her mother and father what she'd seen. Then she told the awful news to Beth and Amy, who both considered it a most agreeable event. Later Laurie came prancing in, bearing a big bouquet for "Mrs. John Brooke."

"You don't look festive," he said to Jo. "What's the matter?"

"You don't know how hard it is for me to give up Meg," she said with a quiver in her voice.

"You don't have to give her up, even though it will never be the same. You've got me, and I'll stand by you, Jo."

"I know you will, Teddy," returned Jo, "and it will be three years till she's twenty," she added thoughtfully.

"Don't you wish you could look forward and see where we all will be then? I do."

A Bouquet for "Mrs. John Brooke"

Mr. March Comes Home to His Books.

Chapter 13
The First Wedding

The three years that passed brought few changes to the family. The war ended, and Mr. March came home to his books.

John Brooke joined the army for a year and then prepared for business and earning a home for Meg.

Meg spent her time working and waiting, and only occasionally felt disappointed at how humble her life was beginning.

Jo never went back to Aunt March. The old lady took a fancy to Amy and offered her drawing lessons as a bribe. Jo devoted herself to writing and to Beth, who remained delicate long after the fever was over. Jo still wrote romances for the newspaper, but she had great plans in her brain.

Laurie went to college to please his grandfather, but did not work hard. He brought home the fellows from his class, and Amy became quite the favorite among them. They all liked Jo, but never fell in love with her.

Mr. Brooke found a tiny, charming house for Meg's first home. It had simple furniture, plenty of books, flowers on the windowsill, and pretty gifts made by the sisters. Jo and her mother put away Meg's few boxes, barrels and bundles. Hannah helped set up the kitchen, and Laurie brought a new gadget every week. The contents of the well-stocked linen closet were from Aunt March, who had not really meant what she said.

On the day before the wedding, Laurie appeared for his weekly visit and reported that

Setting Up Meg's First Home

John had gone for the license and Hannah was just taking in the cake.

Jo and he walked home arm in arm. "Now Teddy," she said, "I want to talk seriously to you about tomorrow. You must promise to behave well. No pranks."

Laurie promised, and Jo sighed, "Well, at least we won't have any more weddings for a while. I think it's dreadful breaking up families."

"Mark my words, you'll go next, Jo," said Laurie.

"No, I'm not the agreeable sort. Nobody will want me."

"You won't give anybody a chance," said Laurie, a little color rising in his cheeks. "When anybody does see the soft side of you, you throw cold water on him."

"I don't like that sort of thing. I'm too busy to be worried with nonsense, so let's change the subject," said Jo crossly.

"You'll be Married Next, Jo."

The wedding day dawned cloudless and rosy. Meg looked like a rose herself. She had made her wedding gown, and the only ornaments she wore were lilies of the valley, John's favorite flower. She rushed about with last minute preparations, but found time to hug each sister.

There was to be no ceremonious performance. Everything was to be as natural and homelike as possible. When Aunt March arrived, she was shocked to see the bride come running to welcome her. Jo upset the cake just as the house was filling with guests.

A silence fell on the room as the couple took their place under the green arch. Mother and sisters gathered close, but Meg looked straight up into her husband's eyes and said, "I will."

Jo did not cry, though she came very close, and only stopped when she felt Laurie's eyes upon her.

Meg Says, "I Will."

The minute after she was married, Meg cried, "The first kiss for Marmee!" and ran to her mother.

There was a lunch of cake and fruit, and then people strolled around through the house and garden. When she was ready to leave, Aunt March said to Meg, "I wish you well, my dear, but I think you'll be sorry for it," and added to the bridegroom, "You've got a treasure, young man, see that you deserve it."

The little house was not far away, and the only bridal journey Meg had was a walk with John from the old house to the new. They all gathered around her to say good-bye.

"I expect to keep my old place in all your hearts even though I am married. You'll all drop in and be with me a great deal. Thank you all for my happy wedding day."

From the Old House to the New

Amy's Artistic Endeavors

Chapter 14
Endeavors

Amy attempted every branch of art with enthusiasm. She devoted herself first to pen and ink drawing, then oil painting, and then charcoal portraits. After this, she went to plaster casts until one day she tried to cast her own foot, and they found her hopping around with her foot in a pan full of hardened plaster. With much difficulty, she was dug out, but Jo was so overcome with laughter, she cut Amy's foot by accident.

Amy was learning, doing and enjoying other things meanwhile, for she had resolved to be an attractive and accomplished woman. She made friends easily and took life gracefully. She had a sense of what was pleasing and proper and knew the right thing to say to each person.

One of her weaknesses, however, was a desire to move in the best society. She considered money, position and elegant manners most desirable, and she and Jo often argued about such questions.

"You don't care to make people like you, or to go into good society. I do, and I mean to make the most of every chance that comes. You can go about with your nose in the air and your elbows out if you like."

Jo did not think herself a genius by any means, but when the "writing fit" came on, she would shut herself in her room and write with her heart and soul. During these periods, the family kept their distance. The writing fits didn't last long, and then she

In a "Writing Fit"

emerged, hungry, sleepy and cross.

Jo attended a lecture one evening and sat next to a lad reading a newspaper. Jo started looking at it, and when he turned the page, the boy offered her half of his paper, saying, "Want to read it? It's a first-rate story."

The story was full of love, mystery, murder and disaster. "I think you or I could do as well if we tried," said Jo, amused that he liked the story so well.

"I would feel pretty lucky if I could! The author of these makes a good living from stories. She knows what folks like and gets paid well for writing it."

Jo took down the address of the paper and resolved to try for the hundred-dollar prize offered for the most sensational story.

She said nothing of her plan, but went to work the next day. She sent off the story and waited for six weeks. When she was just giving up hope, a letter arrived with a check for

Jo Resolves to Try for the Prize.

one hundred dollars. There was a grand jubilee when she told the family.

"What will you do with such a fortune?" asked Amy.

"Send Beth and Mother to the seaside for a month or two!" answered Jo promptly.

To the seaside they went. Beth didn't come back as plump and rosy as could be desired, but she was better. Jo earned several more checks, and the magic of her pen paid the bills and bought a new carpet.

Then Jo decided to submit her novel for publication. In hopes of pleasing everyone, she took all of their advice and ended up suiting nobody. The novel was printed, and she got three hundred dollars for it, but she wasn't satisfied and decided not to write another till she felt ready.

A Grand Jubilee!

Meg's Jelly Won't Jell.

Chapter 15
Domestic Experiences

Right away Meg was determined to be a model housekeeper. One thing she wanted to do was fill her storeroom with homemade preserves. The currants on their bush were ripe, and John sent home jars and sugar. She had seen Hannah make jelly a dozen times, and she spent a long day picking, boiling, and fussing over her jelly. But it wouldn't jell. At five o'clock, Meg sat down in the topsy-turvy kitchen and wept.

It was on this day that John decided to bring a friend home to dinner unannounced.

When they arrived home, there was not a soul around the house. John hurried in, led by the smell of burned sugar.

Meg sobbed dismally in the kitchen. "Oh, John, I'm so tired and hot and cross! I've been at it till I'm worn out."

"Has something dreadful happened?" asked the anxious John.

"The jelly won't jell, and I don't know what to do!" wailed Meg. John laughed and told Meg that he had brought a friend to dinner.

"Take him away at once!" cried Meg. "I can't see him and there isn't any dinner! I meant to go to Mother's!"

"Don't cry," soothed John. "If you lend a hand, everything will be all right. Give us cold meat and bread and cheese; we won't ask for jelly!"

He meant it as a joke, but Meg thought it was cruel. She dropped her apron and went to cry in her room.

A Cruel Joke

When Meg came down, the men had eaten and strolled away together. John came back after seeing his friend off, and they each sat, expecting the other to apologize first.

"Oh, dear," thought Meg, "married life is very trying." But she then decided she would say "forgive me" and went slowly across the room. She kissed her husband on the forehead. Then John said solemnly:

"It was bad of me to laugh at the jelly. I never will again."

In the autumn, Meg and her old friend Sallie, who had married a rich man, spent a lot of time together. Seeing Sallie's pretty things made Meg long for them and pity herself.

Meg knew where John's money was and could take as much as she liked as long as she could account for it once a month in her little account books.

Two days before settling up day, Sallie had been buying silks, and Meg, counting on

Meg Longs for Pretty Things.

twenty-five dollars from Aunt March for New Year's, took twenty-five dollars from the household fund and bought some too. It was a foolish thing to do, and it haunted her.

When John got out his books that night, Meg's heart sank. "Dear John, I'm afraid to show you my book for I've been very extravagant lately. In addition to trifles, I've spent fifty dollars for a silk dress."

For a moment the room was very still.

"I know you are angry, John, but I can't help it. I can't resist when I see Sallie buying all she wants. I try to be contented, but I'm tired of being poor."

The last words were spoken so low she thought he did not hear them. But he did, and they hurt him.

"I was afraid of this, Meg," he said, standing up. "I do my best."

She ran to him and held him close and said she didn't mean it. He forgave her, and the

Settling-Up Day at the Brooke's

next day Meg went to Sallie and told her the truth and asked her to buy the silk as a favor. Sallie did, and then gave it to Meg a while later as a present.

The year rolled around, and then midsummer, and then Meg had twins—a boy and a girl. "Twins, by Jupiter!" was all Laurie could say when he came rushing over. "Isn't it fun? I was never more staggered in my life!"

The boy was named John Laurence, and the girl Margaret, after her mother and grandmother.

"We shall call her Daisy, so as not to have two Megs," said Amy.

"Name him Demijohn, and call him 'Demi' for short!" shouted Laurie.

"Daisy and Demi—just the thing! I knew Teddy would do it," said Jo, clapping her hands. And the babies were known as Daisy and Demi from then on.

Daisy and Demi

Amy Gives Instructions.

Chapter 16
Calls

"Come, Jo, you promised to make calls with me today," said Amy. Jo hated calls of the formal sort and never went until Amy made her.

Jo sighed, but got up to get dressed.

"I'm perfectly miserable, but if you consider me presentable, that's enough."

Amy gave the instructions as they walked:

"The Chesters consider themselves very elegant, so be on your best behavior. Just be calm, cool and quiet—you can do it for fifteen minutes."

Jo took her at her word and sat silent.

Amy tried in vain to make her talk.

"What a haughty, uninteresting girl the elder Miss March is," they heard someone say as they left.

Amy's next instructions to Jo were to be sociable, but she felt anxious, for when Jo turned freakish, there was no knowing when she'd stop.

At the next house, Jo told stories which embarrassed Amy, and in dismay, Amy told her she was washing her hands of Jo.

So Jo enjoyed herself on the next call. There were boys there, and Jo listened to their college stories, sat on the grass, and played with the children.

Their last call was at Aunt March's. Jo wanted to go home, but Amy insisted that they go because Aunt liked it.

Jo said she would show her disapproval of things and people whenever she felt like it, but Amy calmed her down, telling her not to

Jo Enjoys Herself.

worry Aunt with her new ideas.

"I'll try not to," replied Jo, "but I always feel like bursting out with a blunt speech or shocking remark. It's my doom."

They found another aunt, Aunt Carrol, with the old lady. Jo was not in a good mood, but Amy pleased everybody.

During the conversation, Jo said, "I don't like favors, they make me feel like a slave. I'd rather be independent."

"Ahem," coughed Aunt Carrol with a look at Aunt March. Jo sat with her nose in the air.

"Do you speak French, dear?" Aunt Carrol asked Amy later. Amy nodded, but Jo said she couldn't bear French. She thought it a silly language.

Another look passed between the two aunts. Jo brought the visit to an end and shook hands, but Amy kissed both aunts.

A week later, a letter came from Aunt

The Aunts Exchange Looks.

Carrol. She was going abroad soon.

"And she wants me to go with her!" burst in Jo, flying out of her chair.

"No, dear, not you, it's Amy," said Mother.

"Oh, Mother, she's too young! It's my turn first—I *must* go!"

"I'm afraid it's impossible. Aunt says Amy. She says that 'favors burden you' and that you 'hate French.' "

"Oh, my tongue! Why can't I learn to keep it quiet?" moaned Jo.

"Jo dear, I'm very selfish, but I couldn't spare you, and I'm glad you're not going," whispered Beth.

Jo bore up well until Amy left, and she then fled to her attic and cried till she couldn't cry any more.

Amy clung to Laurie at the last minute and he told her, "I'll come and comfort you if anything happens," little dreaming that he would.

Last Minute Fears

A Change in Beth

Chapter 17
Jo's Friend

"Jo, I'm anxious about Beth," said Mrs. March. "It's not her health; it's her spirits. She sits alone and cries a good deal. Now and then I see a look in her face I don't understand."

Jo said thoughtfully, "I think she's growing up. Why, Mother, Beth's eighteen, but we don't realize it. We treat her like a child."

"So we do. I leave Beth to your hands. I depend on you so, Jo," Mrs. March answered.

Jo watched Beth and finally settled on an idea which seemed to explain the change.

One day Beth was watching Laurie go by outside, and Jo saw a tear drop from her eye.

"Mercy on me, Beth loves Laurie!" thought Jo. "Oh, dear, we are growing up. Here's Meg married and a mamma, Amy in Europe, and Beth in love!" She sighed, because everyone in the family felt that Laurie was getting fonder than ever of her. Jo, of course, wouldn't hear of the subject.

Jo watched Laurie that night. Nothing unusual happened—Beth was quiet and Laurie was very kind to her. But Jo thought she saw all kinds of things. Laurie soon sat down next to her.

"Come, Jo, be nice," said Laurie. "After studying all week, I need to be cared for."

"Go to Beth, I'm busy" was her answer.

"No, she's not to be bothered with me. I'd do anything for you, Jo, if you'd let me."

"Now you're flirting," said Jo. "Although you don't see any harm in it, I just can't

"Beth In Love?"

learn how it's done. I've tried, but I don't seem to get on. Not like Amy."

"I'm glad you can't flirt. It's good to see a sensible, straightforward girl who can be both jolly and kind."

"If you must, Teddy," said Jo, dropping her voice, "go and devote yourself to one of the pretty modest girls you do respect."

"I'd rather stay here with you," he said, winding Jo's apron tassel around his finger.

"I thought you hated to be tied to a woman's apron string," Jo retorted.

"That depends on who wears the apron," said Laurie as he fled.

Jo lay awake long that night and was just dropping to sleep when she heard stifled sobs. She flew to Beth's side. "What is it, dear? Is it the old pain?"

"No, it's a new one. But you can't cure it. There is no cure." Beth clung to her sister and cried and then laid her head in Jo's lap.

Tied to Jo's Apron Strings!

Jo was frightened. Even though she thought she knew the cause of Beth's pain, she said:

"Wouldn't it be a comfort to tell me what it is?"

"Not now, not yet."

"Then I won't ask. But remember that Mother and I are always glad to hear and help you."

"I'll tell you by and by," whispered Beth. And so they both went to sleep.

But Jo had made up her mind, and a few days later she told her mother that she wanted to go away for the winter. She needed a change and felt anxious and restless. Jo's idea was to go to New York. Her mother's friend, Mrs. Kirke, had written asking for a young person to teach her children and to sew.

Jo said to her mother slowly, "It may be vain and wrong of me to say it, but—I'm afraid Laurie is getting too fond of me."

"Then you don't care for him in the way he

Jo Comforts Beth.

cares for you?"

"Mercy no! I love the dear boy as I always have, but as for anything more than that, no. I think I had better go away before it comes to anything. Beth can comfort him when I'm gone and cure him of this romantic notion."

Mrs. Kirke gladly accepted Jo. Trembling with fear, she told Laurie about her plans. He took it very quietly and Jo was relieved. But when he said good-bye, he whispered, "It won't do a bit of good, Jo. My eye is on you, so mind what you do."

Mrs. Kirke had a big house and gave Jo the sky parlor, where she could sit and write. The two little girls she was to teach were pretty children.

Soon after Jo arrived, she heard a gentleman with a foreign accent. Later Mrs. Kirke told her that this boarder was Mr. Friedrich Bhaer, from Berlin. He was rather stout, with hair tumbling over his head, a bushy

Mr. Bhaer

beard, kind eyes, and a splendid big voice. He looked like a gentleman though his coat had buttons missing and his shoe was patched.

All the children in the house loved him, and he helped them with their German and often frolicked with them.

Jo spent her days teaching, sewing and writing in her cozy room. She picked up some more bits of news about Mr. Bhaer and was introduced to him by the little girls.

She met him on her way out one day, standing in the doorway of his room holding a sock and a darning needle.

She laughed all the way downstairs, but thought it was sad that he had to mend his own clothes.

Jo met Mr. Bhaer's nephews, Emil and Franz, and thought they were jolly little lads, quite after her own heart.

Mrs. Kirke called Jo one day as she passed Mr. Bhaer's room. "Did you ever see such a

Mr. Bhaer Mends His Own Clothes.

den, my dear? Come and help me. I've been trying to find out what he has done to his handkerchiefs!" Jo went into the topsy-turvy room. Books and papers were everywhere.

"Such a man!" laughed Mrs. Kirke. "I agreed to do his washing and mending, but he forgets to put his things out."

"Let me mend them," said Jo. "He seems to be such a kind man."

So Jo got his things in order and mended all his socks. Nothing was said, but one day Mr. Bhaer came up to her.

"Have you a wish to learn German?"

"Yes," she said, "but you are too busy."

"I have a debt to pay, Miss March." He pointed to the sewing. "You think I'm stupid that I don't see what you do? I have eyes and I see much. Come, a little lesson now and then in return." So they made the bargain.

On New Year's Day, Mr. Bhaer gave Jo a book because he knew she loved books. Not

Straightening Up the Topsy-Turvy Room

having much money, Jo got him several little useful things and put them around his room.

Though very busy, Jo still found time for her writing. Her fondest wish was to fill the house with comforts, give Beth everything she wanted, and go abroad herself. She again took to writing "sensation stories" because they paid well.

She took a story to the *Weekly Volcano*, a paper which printed those kind of stories. The editor agreed to publish it, and he told Jo if she wanted to write more, to make them short and spicy. Her stories filled the columns of the *Weekly Volcano*, but her name never appeared, and she told no one. She was saving the money she got for them to take Beth to the mountains next summer.

Eager to find material for her stories, Jo studied all manner of people, among them, Mr. Bhaer. Everyone liked him, though he was neither great nor handsome. Jo often

Finding a Publisher for Her Stories

watched him, trying to discover his charm. He was always kind, pleasant and cheery. Though poor, he always seemed to be giving something away. He never spoke of himself, and no one ever knew that in his native city he had been a highly respected professor.

Her belief in him strengthened daily. She wanted his respect and friendship. One day when they were having a conversation, it came out that Mr. Bhaer found the papers which printed sensation stories disgusting.

Jo blushed at this, and Mr. Bhaer noticed it. He knew that Jo wrote, but he asked her no questions about her work. He had seen her downtown where the newspaper offices were. And now it suddenly occurred to him that she was doing work she could not be proud of. Jo also felt that she should not be wasting her time writing this trash just because there was a market for it.

When she went to her room, she got out

Mr. Bhaer Doesn't Like Sensation Stories.

her papers and stuffed them into her stove. After that, she wrote no more sensation stories.

Even though she didn't write, she was very busy. It was a long and pleasant winter, and she didn't leave Mrs. Kirke till June.

She said good-bye to Mr. Bhaer warmly. "You won't forget to come and see us, now. I'll never forgive you if you forget, for I want my family to know my friend."

"Do you? Shall I come?" he asked eagerly.

"Yes, come next month. My best friend, Teddy, graduates then. I'm very proud of him." Something in Mr. Bhaer's face changed when her "best friend" was mentioned, and Jo blushed.

That night, after she had gone, he sat before his fire. "I must not hope it now," he said to himself with a sigh, but he was filled with longing.

Jo Burns Her Stories.

"I've Loved You Since I've Known You."

Chapter 18
Heartache

Laurie graduated with honor, and the whole March family and Mr. Laurence were very proud. But the look Laurie gave Jo after the ceremony made her think, "Oh dear! I know he'll say something, and then what shall I do?"

They met on a little path near the river. Dreadful pauses occurred in the conversation. But Jo saw that the moment had come.

"You've got to hear me out, Jo!" Laurie said. "I've loved you ever since I've known you. I've tried to show it, but you wouldn't let me."

"I wanted to save you this," she answered. "I never wanted you to care for me so. That's why I went away. I'm proud and fond of you, but I just can't love you as you want me to."

"Really, truly, Jo?" He took her hands.

"Oh, Teddy, I'm sorry. I can't help it. You know it's impossible for people to love other people if they don't." There was a long pause.

"Don't tell me, Jo, that you love that old man—that professor you were always writing about."

Jo wanted to laugh, but she said, "He isn't old. He's good and kind and the best friend I've got, next to you. I haven't the least idea of loving him or anyone else."

"But you will, and then what shall become of me?"

"You'll love someone else, too, and forget all this," she said sensibly.

Laurie threw himself on the ground, and it was very hard for Jo to continue. "You and I

Jo Tells Laurie the Truth.

are not suited to each other. We would be miserable if we married. So we'll be good friends all our lives. You'll see that I'm right by and by." He shook his head, but she went on. "You'll find some lovely girl. I'm homely and awkward and odd. I don't like elegant society and everything would be horrid! I don't believe I'll ever marry. I'm happy as I am and love my liberty too much."

"I know better!" broke in Laurie.

"I shall always be fond of you, but I'll never marry you!" cried Jo. At this, Laurie broke away, leaving Jo with her hands clasped tightly in her lap.

She went straight to Mr. Laurence and told him the dismal story. Laurie came home composed, went to his piano and played stormily, and then broke off.

"I can't stand this," said the old gentleman and told Laurie he knew. "Take it as a man and don't do anything rash. Why not go

Laurie Plays Stormily.

abroad, as you planned, and forget it?"

"Ah, but I didn't plan to go alone."

"I don't ask you to go alone. I am ready to go anywhere in the world with you."

Laurie hesitated. He knew his grandfather hated traveling. But before he had time to say anything, Mr. Laurence went on, "There is business in London that needs looking after. I've friends I will visit while you tour the continent."

Laurie sighed and then said, "As you like, sir. It doesn't matter where I go or what I do."

Soon they were off. Jo felt very guilty, but Laurie would allow no one to console him. When it came time for them to leave, he kissed each of the girls. Jo followed a minute after to wave a last good-bye. He left without a look behind him, and she knew the boy Laurie would never come back again.

Saying Good-Bye to Laurie

Beth Does Not Get Better.

Chapter 19
Beth's Secret

When Jo came home from Mrs. Kirke's that spring, she was struck with the change in Beth. A heavy weight fell on Jo when she saw her sister's face. It was thinner, and there was a strange transparent look about it.

When she proposed the trip to the mountains, Beth begged not to go so far from home. So Jo and Beth went to the seashore, where Beth could enjoy the open air and fresh sea breezes.

Jo wondered what Beth knew. One day she was looking at the thin cheeks and feeble hands and felt that Beth was drifting away. Beth saw her looking and said, "Oh, Jo, you know now. I've known for a while, but I couldn't tell you. I'm never going to get well."

"Is this what made you so unhappy that you wouldn't let me comfort and help you?" Her heart ached to think of Beth learning to say good-bye to health and love and life.

"It would have been selfish to frighten you," said Beth.

"And I thought you were unhappy because you loved Laurie," Jo confessed.

"How could I when he was so fond of you? I love him dearly, but he will never be anything to me but a brother," said Beth.

"Oh, Beth, you must get well. Nothing else matters," Jo cried. And she held fast to Beth as the sorrow crept over them.

Beth lay thinking a minute and then said, "I don't know how to say it, but I have a feeling that it was never intended I should live

Sorrow Creeps Over the Girls.

long. I'm not like the rest of you. I never had any plans about what I'd do. I couldn't seem to imagine myself as anything but being Beth at home. I never wanted to go away, and the hard part now is leaving you all." Jo could not speak. "I only hope I see Amy again, but she seems so far away."

"She is coming in the spring, and I'm going to have you well and rosy by then," began Jo.

"Jo, don't hope any more. It won't do any good. We'll just enjoy being together now. You'll tell them at home, won't you?"

When they arrived home, there was no need for any words. Beth went right to bed. When Jo came downstairs, her father stood leaning his head on the mantelpiece, and her mother stretched out her arms to Jo for comfort.

No Need for Any Words

"I Thought You'd Never Come!"

Chapter 20
Lazy Laurence

Laurie was in Nice, France, on Christmas Day. A carriage with a single young lady stopped.

"Oh, Laurie, is it you? I thought you'd never come!" cried Amy, holding out both hands.

"I promised to spend Christmas with you, and here I am!"

"I have so much to say I don't know where to begin," said Amy excitedly.

Laurie got into the carriage and Amy watched him. She felt a new sort of shyness, for he was not the merry boy he had been. He was handsomer than ever, but he looked tired and unhappy.

"Beth is doing very poorly, Jo says," Amy began. "I often think I ought to go home."

"No, there's nothing you can do there," he said. Amy had Jo's letter out. Laurie took it, and smiling sadly, he put it in his pocket.

In the meantime, Laurie was also looking at Amy, who was as sprightly and graceful as ever.

Laurie had only intended to stay in Nice a week, but he stayed a month. He was tired of wandering around, and Amy reminded him of home.

Amy made a very good impression on Laurie, but she wondered what had happened to have changed him so.

"I am going out to sketch," said Amy as she joined Laurie one day. When she had settled herself, she asked, "Laurie, when are you going to your grandfather? He expects you,

Laurie Takes Jo's Letter.

and you really should go."

"I only bother him. So I thought I'd stay here and bother you a little longer," he said, lounging near her.

"What would Jo say if she saw you now?" said Amy, hoping to stir him.

"As usual, 'Go away, Teddy, I'm busy.' " He laughed, but it was harsh. Amy caught a new look on Laurie's face—a bitter look, full of pain and regret.

"You are so changed . . . ." but there she stopped. "Well then, tell me what you've heard from home."

"I have nothing to tell."

"Don't you hear often? I thought Jo would write a lot," she said.

Amy did not like him this new way, so she launched into a speech: "I have a new name for you. It's Lazy Laurence. How do you like it?" Her voice was sharp.

"That's not bad."

Lazy Laurence

"Do you want to know what I think of you?" she continued. "Well, I despise you."

Laurie was taken aback. "Why?" he asked.

"Instead of being good, useful and happy, you're lazy and miserable. You have been abroad six months and have done nothing but waste time and disappoint your friends. You are much worse since you left home."

The lecture had some effect, for Laurie's eyes sparkled, he sat up, and held out his hand.

Then Amy noticed that he wore the small ring Jo had given him long ago, and she suddenly knew. Laurie never spoke of Jo. She recalled the shadow that had passed over his face a moment ago. Amy had thought that maybe love was the cause of his problems, but now she was sure.

"Laurie," she began in her sweetest voice, "they ought to have told me. Did that girl you liked, Miss Randall, break—"

Amy Lectures Laurie.

"No, it wasn't her. You know perfectly well I never cared for anyone but Jo," said Laurie turning his face away. "If I'm a good-for-nothing, it's her fault, and you may tell her."

"I'm sorry, Teddy dear—"

"Don't! That's her name for me." He pulled at the grass. Presently he said, "Do you think Jo would despise me as you do?"

"Yes, if she saw you now. She hates lazy people. If you'd set upon a task, you'd soon be your happy, hearty self again."

"That's impossible!"

"Try it and see" was Amy's advice.

Neither spoke for several minutes, and Amy felt a shade of coldness in his manner, but was glad she had said what she did.

Next morning, instead of his usual call, she found a note. It said that "Lazy Laurence" had gone to his grandpa.

"I'm glad he's gone," said Amy, but added with a sigh, "I shall miss him."

A Note for Amy

A Pleasant Room for Beth

Chapter 21
The Valley of the Shadow

The family accepted that Beth was not going to get well. They tried to bear it cheerfully.

The most pleasant room in the house was set apart for Beth, and in it they gathered everything she most loved. Nothing changed her nature, and the first few months were happy ones.

But by and by, Beth said her needle was "so heavy" and she put it down. Talking wearied her. Long nights followed heavy days.

Jo never left her for an hour. She slept on

a couch in the room. Often when she woke, she found Beth reading or singing softly while slow tears dropped through her fingers.

One night Beth looked among the books on her table and found a little paper scribbled in Jo's hand. It was a poem about her. Beth's one regret was that she had done so little, but the poem seemed to assure her that her life had not been useless.

When Jo came to her bedside, Beth said, "It's such a comfort to know that someone loves me as much as you do. You must take my place, Jo, and be everything to Mother and Father when I'm gone."

The spring days came, and the birds came back to say good-bye to Beth. In the dark hour before the dawn, she drew her last breath with one loving look, one sigh.

When morning came, for the first time in many months, the fire was out and Beth's room was empty.

A Dark Hour

Thoughts of Amy

Chapter 22
Learning to Forget

Laurie kept remembering Amy's words: "Go and do something splendid that will make her love you." Mr. Laurence noted a change, and Laurie admitted he had been selfish and lazy.

He decided to put his sorrow in love into music, but instead caught himself humming dancing tunes from the Christmas ball he had gone to with Amy. He knew a change was going on in spite of himself.

Laurie thought that forgetting Jo would take years, but to his great surprise, it grew easier every day. His love for Jo slowly changed to tender affection. He received a letter from her saying that Beth was worse and telling him to write Amy often so she would not feel lonely or homesick.

So he did write to Amy, but he also took off Jo's little ring from his finger and locked it in the drawer with her letters.

Amy answered Laurie's letter right away, and letters flew back and forth between them. He wanted to see her, but she didn't ask him. She grew pale and thoughtful.

While these changes were going on abroad, trouble had come at home. The sad news of Beth's death met Amy at Vevay, in Switzerland. She bore it very well, but her heart was heavy, and she longed to be at home. Laurie was in Germany when he heard the news, and he set off immediately to comfort Amy.

He knew Vevay well and hurried to Amy. She was sitting in the garden, thinking of

Laurie Rushes to Comfort Amy.

Beth and wondering why Laurie didn't come. She did not hear him cross the courtyard, but the minute she looked up she ran to him saying, "Oh, Laurie, I knew you'd come to me!"

Amy felt no one could comfort her as well as Laurie, and Laurie decided that Amy was the only woman in the world who could fill Jo's place. For an hour they walked and talked, and Amy felt her loneliness and sorrow lift.

The moment Aunt Carrol saw Amy's face, she thought, "Now I understand—the child has been pining for young Laurence."

The Swiss air did them both good, and in spite of the sorrow, it was a happy time.

There was no need for Laurie to tell Amy he loved her. She knew it without words.

While rowing on the lake one day, he asked her if she would be his, and she answered, "Yes, Laurie."

A Marriage Proposal

Dark Days for Jo

Chapter 23
All Alone

These were dark days for Jo, and she was filled with despair at the thought of spending all her days in that quiet house. Often she started up at night, thinking Beth had called, but her mother came to comfort her, and her father was there in the study when she wanted to talk.

As they sat sewing, she saw how happy her sister Meg was. Jo loved the babies tenderly, and Meg saw a glimmer of Jo's old spirit when they were around.

"Why don't you write? That always used to

make you happy," said her mother one day.

"I've no heart to write," answered Jo. "Nobody cares for my things anyway."

"We do," said her mother. "Write something for us. I'm sure it would do you good."

An hour afterward, her mother peeped in and found Jo scratching away. Her father sent Jo's story—much against her will—to a magazine, which paid for it and requested others. For a small thing, it was a great success. So Jo wrote more stories.

When Amy and Laurie wrote of their engagement, Mrs. March feared Jo would not be able to rejoice over it. Though Jo looked grave at first, she was full of hopes for "the children." Mrs. March said she had suspected it all along, but hadn't wanted to suggest to Jo that her Teddy loved someone else. "Forgive me, dear," Mrs. March added, "I can't help seeing that you are lonely, and I wondered if he came back and asked again if you

Jo Tries Writing Again.

might give a different answer."

"No, Mother," said Jo. But she went back and read the letter again and sighed, "How very happy they must be."

Then she went up to her garret and cried, wondering why one sister should have all she asked, and the other nothing. She drew out some notebooks she had written at Mrs. Kirke's, and her eye caught on a little message written in Professor Bhaer's hand.

"Oh, how I should love to see him. My dear Friedrich, I didn't value him half enough when I had him."

One evening Jo was alone on the sofa thinking. Her face looked tired and grave. She had fallen asleep and was awakened by Laurie as he stooped down to kiss her. She flew up crying, "Oh, my Teddy!"

"Dear Jo, are you glad to see me?"

"Oh, yes, and where's Amy?"

Jo Longs to See Her Friend.

"Your mother has got my wife down at Meg's," Laurie replied.

"Your *what?*" cried Jo. "You've gone and got married!"

"Yes," he said, going on his knees, "the one and only time! I wanted to be the one to tell you."

"Why didn't you let us know?"

"We wanted to surprise everyone!" he said, and then they settled down for a good talk, for Jo wanted to hear the whole story. Laurie then took her hand and said, "Jo, dear, I want to say one thing, and then we'll put it aside forever. I shall never stop loving you, but the love is changed. I was a boy when I first loved you, and I made a fool of myself. But will you now go back to the happy old times we used to have?"

"We can't go back and mustn't expect to. I see the change in you, and you'll find it in me. But we will be brother and sister, and

A Great Surprise!

help one another all our lives."

Jo didn't want the homecoming to be sad, but Laurie said, "Poor Jo, we left you to bear it alone. You *are* older, and your eyes are sad. You've had a great deal to bear."

"No, I had help. I am lonely sometimes, but—"

"You shall never be again," broke in Laurie. "Amy and I can't get on without you, and we'll all be happy and friendly together."

But then Amy's voice was heard calling, "Where is she? Where is my dear old Jo?"

In trooped the whole family, and everyone was hugged and kissed all over again. Amy's face was full of brightness, and everyone made much of the three travelers, for they had been gone three years. They had tea, and then everyone went upstairs except Jo, who felt a sudden sense of loneliness come over her. For even her Teddy had deserted her.

But then there came a knock at the door.

All Together Again

She opened it and started as if another ghost had come to surprise her. There stood a tall bearded gentleman.

"Oh, Mr. Bhaer, I am so glad to see you," cried Jo, clutching him.

"And I to see Miss March."

"Come in, my sister and friends have just come home, and we are all very happy." She couldn't hide her joy at seeing him, and the welcome gave him hope.

"Have you been ill, my friend?" he asked abruptly, for the light fell on Jo's face, and he saw a change in it.

"Not ill, but tired and sorrowful."

"Ah, yes, I know. I heard." They shook hands again, and Jo felt comforted.

Mr. Bhaer received a warm welcome up-stairs. The twins went to him at once, and the women looked on with approval. Laurie stood aloof, feeling a twinge—not of jealousy, but of suspicion—but it did not last long.

Another Surprise

Mr. Bhaer's face looked alive with interest, actually young and handsome, Jo thought. He was dressed in a new black suit. Nothing about him escaped Jo, who sat knitting away quietly. "Dear old fellow! He couldn't have got himself up better if he'd been going courting," said Jo to herself, and then she blushed at her thought.

Everyone sat around the fire talking until Meg finally made a move to go. "We must have our sing, for we are all together again," said Jo. But even though they were not *all* there, Beth still seemed among them.

"I too shall go," Mr. Bhaer said, "but I will gladly come again, for a little business will keep me in the city a few days." He spoke to Mrs. March, but looked at Jo.

Jo wondered what business had brought Mr. Bhaer to the city. She would have known if she could have seen how, later in his room, he looked at a picture of her.

Mr. Bhaer Has Come "On Business."

Caught in the Rain

Chapter 24
Under the Umbrella

By the second week Mr. Bhaer was there, everyone knew perfectly well what was going on. The Professor's hat was on the March's hall table nearly every evening, and Jo sang as she went about her work and did up her hair four times a day.

But then Mr. Bhaer stayed away for three days. Jo was very cross as she set out for her daily walk one dull afternoon. She went the long way and soon felt a drop of rain on her cheek. "It serves me right," she said to herself as she got wetter, "to put on my best things and wander about, hoping to see the Professor." She was rushing across the street when she heard a voice:

"You have no umbrella!" Mr. Bhaer smiled and held his over her head.

"We thought you had gone," said Jo hastily, trying to keep her voice calm.

"Do you think I would go without saying good-bye to those who have been so kind? No, I will come one more time before I go."

"You *are* going then?"

"I no longer have any business here. My friends have found a place for me at a college, where I will teach as I did in Germany."

"How splendid!" cried Jo.

"Ah, but I fear this place is not near here. It is in the west."

"So far away!" said Jo, her face falling.

Mr. Bhaer grew more hopeful at her exclamation. Walking home, Jo's feet were cold, but her heart felt colder. Mr. Bhaer was

Mr. Bhaer Holds the Umbrella.

going away, he only cared for her as a friend. A few tears fell from her eyes.

Mr. Bhaer saw them and asked, "Dearest heart, why do you cry?"

"Because you are going away," Jo answered in a most undignified way.

"Jo," cried Mr. Bhaer, clasping his hands, "I came to see if you could care for me. I wanted to be sure I was more than a friend. Am I?"

"Oh, yes!" said Jo happily. "Friedrich," she added bashfully, "why didn't you tell me sooner?"

"I had a wish to tell you when I said good-bye in New York, but I thought you were in love with your handsome friend."

"Teddy was only a boy and soon got over his little fancy," said Jo. "But I don't know if I would have said yes then. You came just when I wanted you."

"Although my heart is full, I cannot take

More Than a Friend

you from your happy home till I have one to give you. Have you patience? I must go away and do my work alone and care for my nephews. Can you be happy while we hope and wait?"

"Yes, I can, for we love one another." Then Jo, who never would learn to be proper, kissed her Friedrich under the umbrella.

For a year Jo and her professor worked and waited, met occasionally, and wrote many long letters.

In the beginning of the second year, Aunt March died, and she left her large house to Jo. She and Friedrich decided to open a school for boys.

"I've always longed for boys, and now I can fill a whole house with them! Friedrich will teach, and Father will help too. And we'll all help with the work."

Almost before she knew where she was, Jo found herself married and settled. The school flourished and was filled with poor boys as

A School Filled with Boys

well as rich.

It was hard work, and they never became rich from it. Jo was a happy woman in spite of the work and the constant racket. As the years went on, she had two little lads of her own—Rob, named for Grandpa, and Teddy, a happy-go-lucky baby with his father's sunshiny disposition.

Five years after Jo's wedding, the Marches, the Brookes, the Laurences and the Bhaers all gathered in the orchard for apple-picking. Meg, Jo and Amy sat under the tree with their mother, thinking about the life they had pictured for themselves long ago. Then Mrs. March stretched out her arms, gathering her children to her. She smiled and said:

"Oh, my girls, however long you live, I never can wish you a greater happiness than this."

No Greater Happiness Than This